THE WORLD CUP

KURT WALDENDORF

childsworld.com

The Child's World
childsworld.com

Published by The Child's World®
800-599-READ • childsworld.com

Photography Credits
Cover: ©Julian Finney/Getty Images; ©AlexeyVS/Getty Images; page 4: ©irin-k/Shutterstock; page 5: ©Rischgitz/Getty Images; page 6: ©PA Images/Getty Images; page 9: ©Bettmann/Getty Images; page 10: ©George Rinhart/Getty Images; page 11: ©ShanDiam/Shutterstock; ©Martial Red/Shutterstock; page 13: ©Keystone/Getty Images; page 14: ©EMPICS/Newscom; page 15: ©Staff/Getty Images; page 16: ©pham vecdesign/Shutterstock; page 17: ©Keystone/Getty Images; page 19: ©Tommy Cheng/Getty Images; page 20: picture-alliance/dpa/Newscom; page 21: ©Daniela Porcelli/ISI Photos/Getty Images; page 23: ©picture alliance/Getty Images; page 24: ©Ben Radford/Getty Images; page 25: ©El Grafico/Getty Images; page 26: ©Roberto Schmidt/Getty Images; page 28: ©Gina Ferazzi/Getty Images; page 29: ©Dedert Arne/DPA/ABACA/Newscom

ISBN Information
ISBN 9781503894266 (Reinforced Library Binding)
ISBN 9781503895287 (Portable Document Format)
ISBN 9781503896109 (Online Multi-user eBook)
ISBN 9781503896925 (Electronic Publication)

LCCN
2024941411

Printed in the United States of America

ABOUT THE AUTHOR

Kurt Waldendorf is the author of more than a dozen books for children. When he's not writing or editing, he enjoys indoor rock climbing and running along the shores of Lake Michigan with his dog. He lives in Chicago.

CONTENTS

CHAPTER ONE

EARLY INTERNATIONAL SOCCER

Soccer, which is called "football" in most countries, is a global game. More than 200 countries have national teams. Each of these teams is made up of a country's top players. Every four years, national teams compete against one another in the World Cup. The winner of this tournament is named world champion. Today, the World Cup is one of the most popular sporting events in the world. But it took many years to become what it is now.

International soccer started small. The first matchups took place in the United Kingdom (UK). The UK includes England, Scotland, Wales, and Northern Ireland. In 1863, a group called the Football Association (FA) created standard rules for soccer. With standard rules, the sport spread quickly across the UK. A **rivalry** began between England and Scotland. In 1872, top players from the two countries faced off. The match took place in Glasgow, Scotland, in front of almost 4,000 people. The match ended in a draw, or tie.

As early as 1872, soccer was so popular that local newspapers often reported on games. This image was included with a story about a game between England and Scotland.

Around 32,000 people gathered to watch England and Scotland play in the British International Championship. The tournament was the oldest international tournament in soccer history.

Soccer continued to spread in the late 1800s. Transportation was getting better during this time. This made it easier for teams to travel to play each other. Teams from Wales and Scotland faced off in 1876. Scotland won 4–0. Northern Ireland played its first match against England in 1882. England won 13–0.

Meanwhile, sailors and immigrants brought soccer to other countries. One of the first matches in North America took place in 1885 in Newark, New Jersey. The United States and Canada played. The Canadians won 1–0. In South America, the first international match was in 1902. Argentina beat Uruguay 6–0. The same year, Austria beat Hungary 5–0 in the first international match in Europe.

In 1904, an international soccer organization formed. It was called the Fédération Internationale de Football Association (**FIFA**). FIFA continues to oversee international soccer to this day.

CHAPTER TWO

THE RISE OF THE OLYMPICS

As soccer became a global game, the sport's organizers thought there should be a global tournament. They turned to the Olympics. The Summer Olympic Games are held every four years. They feature top athletes across many different sports. Starting in 1908, countries sent their national soccer teams to compete. Early on, England dominated. The country where modern soccer began won the gold medals in 1908 and 1912.

However, the sport did not catch on quickly at the Olympics. In 1908, only six teams competed. The 1912 games featured 11 teams. All the teams were from Europe. In addition, the Olympics did not allow **professional** players to take part. This rule was meant to keep the focus on sports rather than on money. But it also kept some countries from sending teams.

The 1924 tournament included more teams. Egypt, Turkey, Uruguay, and the United States all took part. Uruguay made a memorable first appearance. The team won gold and finished without a loss.

England and Scotland were two of the world's first soccer rivals. The two teams have played more than 100 matches in their history.

Soccer was one of the first team sports to be included in the Olympic Games.

In 1928, Mexico and Argentina took part for the first time. In all, 17 countries competed. In the **final**, Uruguay beat Argentina 2–1 for the country's second gold medal. The match drew more than 25,000 fans. For the first time, soccer was the most popular sport at the Olympics. Because of the larger number of teams, people call the 1928 Olympics the first world championship of soccer.

Though the tournament was a success, members of FIFA were not pleased. They did not like the rule that kept pro athletes from playing. FIFA began planning its own tournament. The World Cup was born.

CHAPTER THREE

THE FIRST WORLD CUP

FIFA president Jules Rimet started planning the World Cup in 1926. FIFA decided the first tournament would take place in 1930. That way, it would happen between the Summer Olympic Games. Unlike the Olympics, it would be open to all athletes, both pro and **amateur**.

In 1928, FIFA said that Uruguay would host the tournament. Uruguay had won gold medals in the last two Olympic games. The country also offered to pay for teams to travel to the event, making it a strong choice to host. The games would be played in the country's capital, Montevideo. At the time, FIFA had 41 member nations. All were invited to participate in the first World Cup. But bringing the nations together in a single place was a difficult task.

Until 1974, the World Cup trophy was also called the Jules Rimet Trophy after the founder of the World Cup tournament.

Uruguay's Centennial Stadium, or Estadio Centenario, was built for the 1930 World Cup. The stadium has been updated and is still in use.

Many South American countries were quick to sign up. So were Mexico and the United States. Other countries were hesitant. The trip to South America would be long for many national teams. In addition, the event took place during the **Great Depression**. During this time, countries struggled financially. Many players had jobs other than soccer. They could not risk being away for so long.

Japan and Thailand decided not to participate. England, Italy, Spain, and Germany also chose not to send teams. In the end, only 14 countries agreed to make the trip. For European teams such as Belgium, France, Romania, and Yugoslavia, the journey took more than two weeks by boat. The ship carrying the Egyptian team got caught in a storm. The team had to turn back. In July 1930, 13 teams arrived in Montevideo for the World Cup.

The French National Team spent 14 days at sea on their way to the 1930 World Cup in Uruguay.

During the first round of matches, players faced other difficulties. It was winter in Uruguay, making it cold and rainy. It even snowed during one game, a rare occurrence in Uruguay. Despite the conditions, players made history. Lucien Laurent scored the first World Cup goal in France's match against Mexico. American Bert Patenaude notched three goals in a match against Paraguay. It was the World Cup's first **hat trick**.

1930 WORLD CUP BRACKET

Semifinals

27 July – Montevideo

Team	Score
Uruguay	6
Yugoslavia	1

26 July – Montevideo

Team	Score
Argentina	6
United States	1

Finals

30 July – Montevideo

Team	Score
Uruguay	4
Argentina	2

Although Argentina scored two goals against Uruguay's goalkeeper during the 1930 World Cup final, the host country won the tournament 4–2.

In the final, Uruguay faced off against Argentina. The contest was a repeat of the 1928 Olympic final, which Uruguay had won. Around 15,000 fans traveled from Argentina to see the match. On game day, 93,000 people filled the stadium. They saw the host country beat Argentina 4–2. In all, more than 400,000 people came to watch the 1930 World Cup matches. Even with its difficult beginnings, the first World Cup was a big success.

CHAPTER FOUR

A CHANGING TOURNAMENT

After the first World Cup, the tournament grew and changed. The 1934 tournament included a **qualifying** round for the first time. This round takes place before the World Cup. Teams from each **confederation** compete. The top teams from each confederation earn a spot in the tournament.

In 1958, more changes came. The tournament included 16 teams divided into four groups. Each member of the group played against the others. The top two teams from each group advanced to the next round. The group stage's **round-robin** format was popular with fans. It gave teams more chances to prove themselves before being eliminated.

As more countries joined FIFA, the men's tournament continued to grow. The women's game was also growing. So FIFA created the Women's World Cup. This tournament takes place one year after the men's tournament. The Women's World Cup began in 1991 with 12 teams. It grew to 16 teams in 1999 and to 24 in 2015.

The 1991 Women's World Cup was held more than 60 years after the first men's tournament took place.

NO CHAMPIONSHIP GAME

The 1950 World Cup was unique. It was the only time the event did not have a championship match. Instead, the winners of the group stage played in a second round-robin tournament. The team with the most victories was the champion. Fans did not like this. In 1954, the tournament went back to having a championship match.

Today, the World Cup continues to change. In 2023, the women's tournament grew to 32 teams. On the men's side, FIFA voted in 2017 to expand the 2026 World Cup to 48 teams. FIFA announced the tournament would be hosted by three countries: Mexico, the United States, and Canada.

In 2030, FIFA will celebrate the World Cup's 100th anniversary. FIFA has big plans for the occasion. The men's tournament will take place across three continents and six countries. In Africa, matches will take place in Morocco. In Europe, Portugal and Spain will host. In South America, players will suit up in Uruguay, Argentina, and Paraguay. The first match will take place in Uruguay. Fans will pack the same stadium where the World Cup began 100 years earlier.

The 2023 World Cup win was the first for the Spain Women's National Team.

CHAPTER FIVE

WORLD CUP MOMENTS

At the World Cup, the best players in the world compete on the biggest stage. As a result, some of soccer's greatest moments have taken place at the event. Two of these happened in the 1970 Men's World Cup in Mexico. At the time, Brazil's star, Pelé, was the top player in the world. In a match against England, he **headed** the ball toward an open net. It looked like an easy goal. But English goalkeeper Gordon Banks moved quickly. He knocked the ball over the crossbar. England eventually lost the match. But Banks's effort became known as the "save of the century."

Then, in the final, Pelé and the Brazilian team made a great moment of their own. Nine Brazilian players passed the ball before scoring the winning goal. The excellent teamwork led people to call it "the perfect goal."

Brazil's 1970 World Cup win was the country's third. They have won the tournament twice since then.

A CHANGING RIVALRY

The US men's team has never won a World Cup. But in 2002, the team scored a big win. The US squad took on its biggest rival, Mexico. For years, Mexico had dominated the matchup. But when the United States won a surprising 2–0 victory, things began to change. Over the next 25 matchups, the United States went 11 and 8 against Mexico, with 6 draws.

Two more memorable moments came in the 1986 World Cup. This time, Argentina's Diego Maradona was the top player. In a match against England, he scored two famous goals. The first came in the 51st minute. Maradona leaped to head the ball into the net. The English goalkeeper leaped even higher to knock the ball away. Somehow, the ball ended up in the net. The English side said Maradona punched the ball in with his hand. But the goal stood. It is one of the most **controversial** moments in World Cup history. Soccer fans call it the "Hand of God" goal.

Later in the game, Maradona scored again. This time, there was no controversy. He took the ball at midfield. He weaved past four defenders. Finally, he leaped around the goalkeeper and struck the ball into the net. Due to Maradona's skill, the goal is known as the "goal of the century."

Technology at the 1986 World Cup was not as advanced as it is today. The referees could not ask to see replays of goals or fouls like they do in modern times. Today, Maradona's (left) goal probably would not be allowed.

Brandi Chastain's winning shot in the 1999 Women's World Cup is one of the tournament's most memorable moments. Chastain and her teammates paved the way for a new generation of soccer fans and players.

In the Women's World Cup, the United States has had many of the top moments. One came at the end of the 1999 final. After a scoreless draw, the match came down to **penalty kicks**. US star Brandi Chastain calmly set the ball in place. Then, after striking the game-winning kick, she erupted in celebration. She flexed and waved her jersey in the air. The moment gave the US its second title. It also inspired a new generation of US players.

One of those players was Carli Lloyd. In 2015, Lloyd had an amazing moment of her own. In the final against Japan, she scored three goals in the game's first 16 minutes. It was the second-fastest hat trick in World Cup history. Lloyd's effort led the Americans to a third title.

GOLDEN GOAL

Another top moment occurred at the 2003 Women's World Cup. In the final, Germany took on Sweden. The match went into extra time. According to the "golden goal" rule, the first team to score would be the winner. So when Germany's Nia Künzer knocked in a goal just eight minutes into extra time, the match was over. It was the only time a World Cup had been decided by a "golden goal." FIFA got rid of the rule after the tournament.

Teams other than the United States have also had top moments at the Women's World Cup. In 2011, Japan faced off against the United States in the final. The match took place just months after a terrible earthquake had struck Japan. In the match, Japan stunned the world, winning in penalty kicks. For the people of Japan, it wasn't simply the first time their country had won a title. The win was also a sign of hope during a difficult time.

Today, the sport of soccer continues to grow. The World Cup is growing, too. As the tournament expands, more players have the chance to make great moments. When they do, they contribute to the legend of the tournament and make their countries proud.

With their first World Cup win in 2011, Japan became the fourth country to win the women's tournament. Spain became the fifth in 2023.

GLOSSARY

amateur (AM-uh-chur) taking part in a sport for pleasure, not for pay

confederation (kuhn-fed-uh-RAY-shuhn) a governing body formed by uniting smaller bodies

controversial (kon-truh-VUR-shuhl) causing public disagreement

FIFA (FEE-fah) short for Fédération Internationale de Football Association; the group that oversees international soccer

final (FY-nul) the last or championship game or match of a tournament that determines the event's winner

Great Depression (GRAYT dih-PRESH-uhn) a time of hard economic conditions, in which many people were out of work, hungry, or homeless

hat trick (HAT TRIK) the scoring of three goals in one match by one player

headed (HEH-did) used one's head to direct the ball

penalty kicks (PEN-uhl-tee KIKS) free kicks taken at the goal after teams commit fouls or to decide a match's winner after extra time

professional (proh-FESH-uh-nahl) taking part in a sport for money

qualifying (KWAL-ih-fy-ing) games played to determine which players or teams will compete in a tournament, such as the World Cup or Olympics

rivalry (RY-vuhl-ree) a competition for superiority between two teams

round-robin (ROWND RAH-bin) a competition in which every contestant plays once against every other contestant

FAST FACTS

- The stadium built for the first World Cup was not completed until five days into the tournament.
- World Cup tournaments have taken place on every continent except Antarctica.
- Due to World War II, no World Cups took place in 1942 or 1946.
- Brazil is the only country to have taken part in every Men's World Cup.
- The fastest World Cup goal took place 11 seconds into a match.
- The 2022 World Cup used a "smart ball," making the ball's exact position known at all times.

ONE STRIDE FURTHER

- What were some of the challenges organizers of the first World Cup faced? Write a paragraph describing what it took for the event to be a success.
- What does it take to create a top soccer moment? Make a list and have a friend do the same. Compare your lists.
- Ask friends and family members about their favorite sports. Keep track and make a graph to see which sport wins out.

FIND OUT MORE

IN THE LIBRARY

Davidson, B. Keith. *MLS*. New York, NY: Crabtree, 2022.

Everything You Need to Know about Soccer. New York, NY: DK Children, 2024.

Lowe, Alexander. *G.O.A.T. Soccer Midfielders*. Minneapolis, MN: Lerner, 2022.

Lowe, Alexander. *G.O.A.T. Soccer Strikers*. Minneapolis, MN: Lerner, 2022.

ON THE WEB

Visit our website for links about the World Cup:

childsworld.com/links

Note to Parents, Caregivers, Teachers, and Librarians: We routinely verify our web links to make sure they are safe and active sites. So encourage your readers to check them out!

INDEX